Divine Designs Jubilee
Using God's Word to Encourage

A creative faith based inspired collection
to celebrate love, harmony, hope, joy and life.

Dr. Suzan Dian Seger

Copyright © 2024 Dr. Suzan Dian Seger.

All rights reserved. No part of this book may be used or reproduced by any means, graphic, electronic, or mechanical, including photocopying, recording, taping or by any information storage retrieval system without the written permission of the author except in the case of brief quotations embodied in critical articles and reviews.

Balboa Press books may be ordered through booksellers or by contacting:

Balboa Press
A Division of Hay House
1663 Liberty Drive
Bloomington, IN 47403
www.balboapress.com
844-682-1282

Because of the dynamic nature of the Internet, any web addresses or links contained in this book may have changed since publication and may no longer be valid. The views expressed in this work are solely those of the author and do not necessarily reflect the views of the publisher, and the publisher hereby disclaims any responsibility for them.

Any people depicted in stock imagery provided by Getty Images are models, and such images are being used for illustrative purposes only.
Certain stock imagery © Getty Images.

Interior Image Credit: Dr. Suzan Dian Seger

Scripture quotations marked NIV are taken from the Holy Bible, New International Version®. NIV®. Copyright © 1973, 1978, 1984 by International Bible Society. Used by permission of Zondervan. All rights reserved. [Biblica]

ISBN: 979-8-7652-5396-0 (sc)
ISBN: 979-8-7652-5395-3 (e)

Library of Congress Control Number: 2024915205

Print information available on the last page.

Balboa Press rev. date: 07/31/2024

Dedication

First and foremost, praises to the Lord, my God. I will give Him thanks forever. "To God be all the glory for all of the great things He has done in my life. I am truly thankful. I will praise the Lord at all times and I will constantly speak His praises" Psalm 34:1.

This book is dedicated to the three most significant people in my lifetime on this Earth: my mom, my son, and my daughter.

In loving memory of my wonderful mom, Louella Patricia Barnes Seger, who was truly the most influential person in my entire life and from whom I received my spunk, perseverance and determination. Her words of wisdom, love of God and gardening, home remedies, gumption, tenacity, and strong work ethic continue to inspire me daily. Mom encouraged my creativity and my continued education, saying that, "It was something that no one could ever take away from me."

No love on earth can ever compare to the love of a mom, and she will remain in my heart forever.

To my precious children, Adam and Sarah, thank you, thank you, thank you from the bottom of my heart for your faithful love, encouragement and support. You are truly God's gift to me; you are my heart, my soul and my priority, forever. I love you both dearly! I appreciate and respect you completely. You make me proud every single day. Being your mom has been the highest calling for me on this Earth. "Children are a gift from God" Psalm 127:3.

Love Diversity

God shows no partiality In His eyes we are all one

Acts 10:34

Remain true to your Faith

Acts 14:22

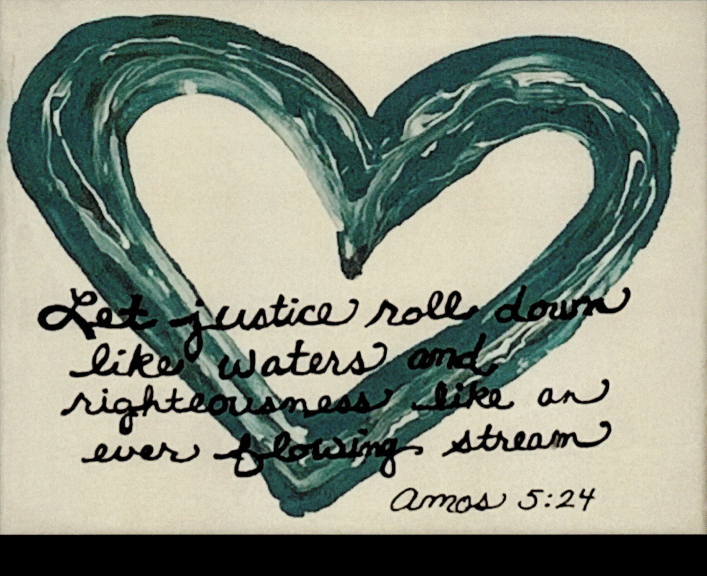

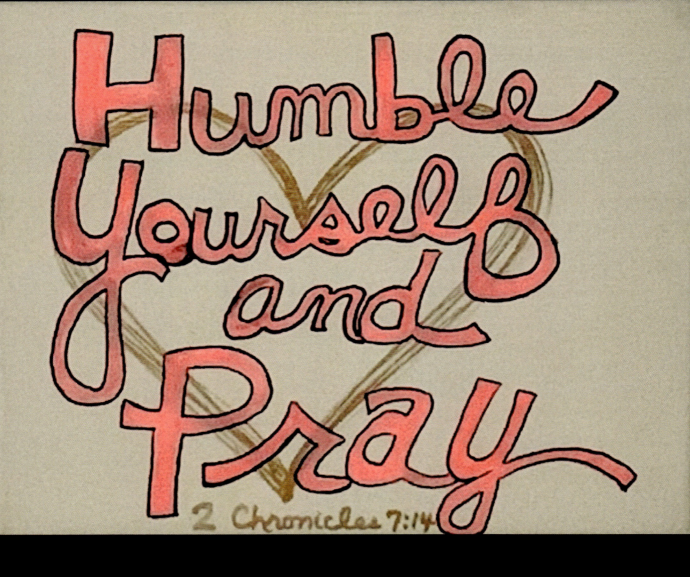

Overflowing with Thankfulness

Colossians 2:7

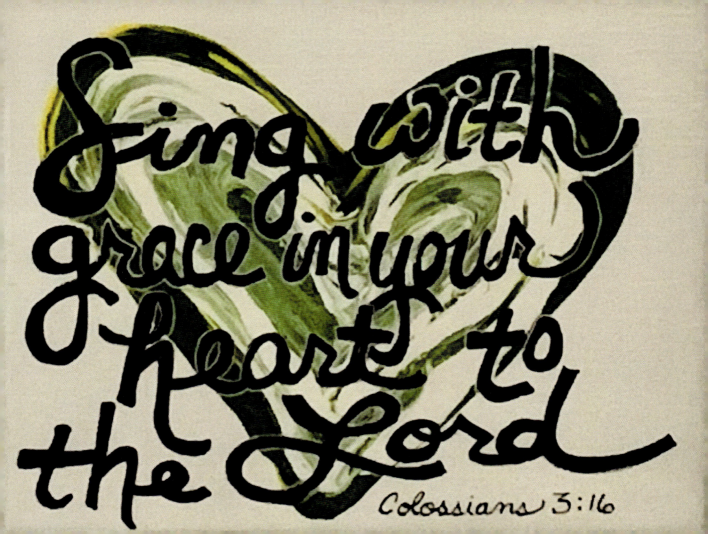

Hope

Faith Hope Love

1 Corenthians 13

The Lord will be with you. He will never leave you nor forsake you.

Deuteronomy 31:8

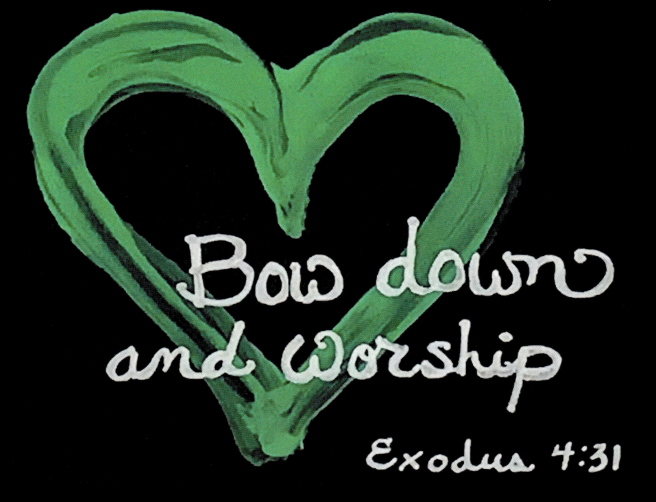

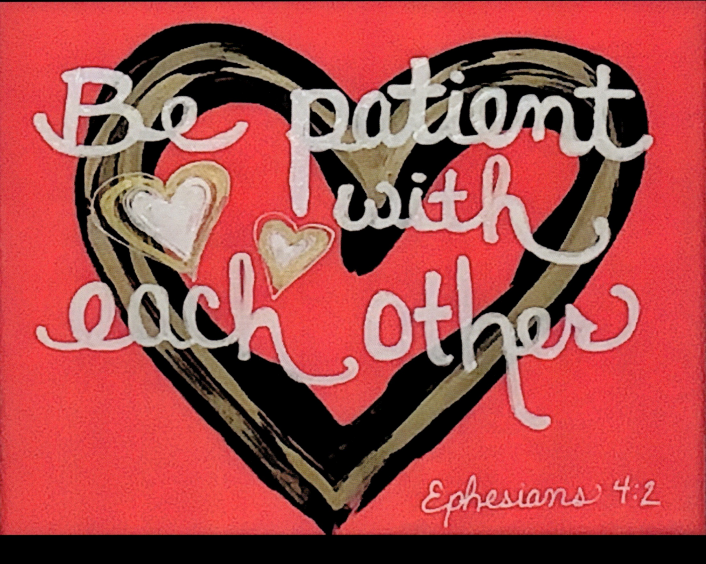

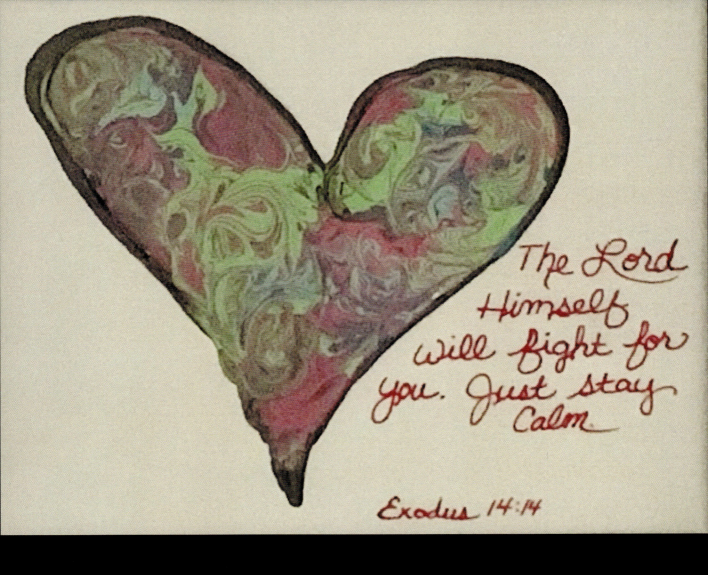

A cord of three strands is not easily broken

Ecclesiastes 4:12

He set a royal crown on her head

Ester 2:17

The Lord is good His Loving Kindness Endures Forever

Ezra 3:11

all the glory to God

Galatians 1:5

He will bestow on them a crown
of beauty instead of ashes
The oil of joy instead of mourning
and a garment of praise
instead of a spirit of despair

— Isaiah 61:3

Give careful thought to your ways says the Lord Almighty

Haggai 1:7

Honor the Lord in your Home

Haggai 1:8

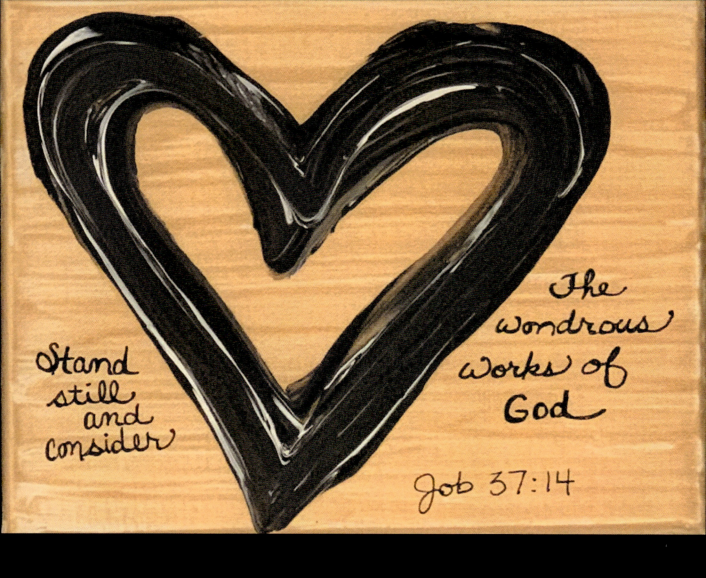

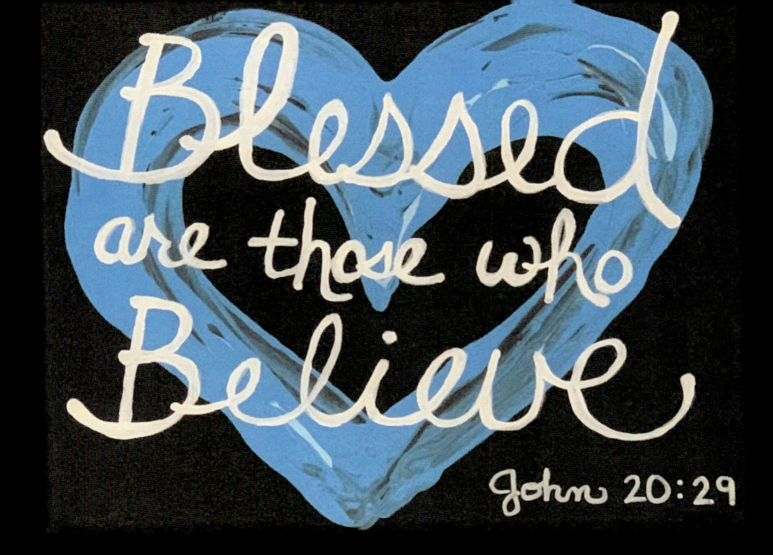

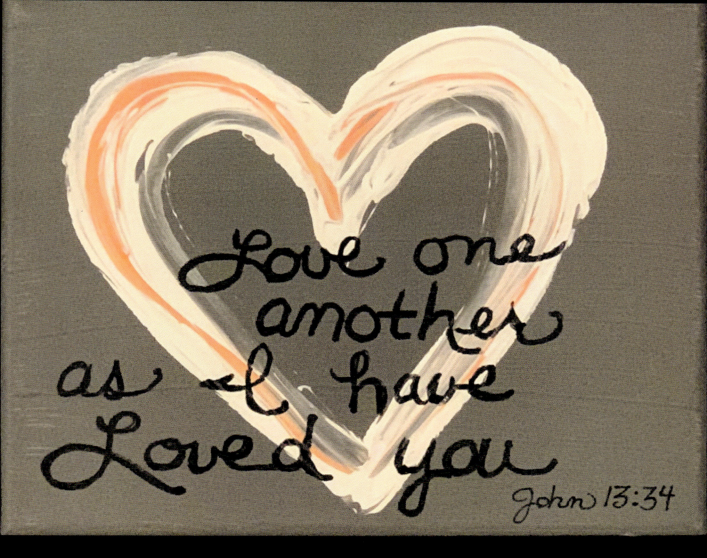

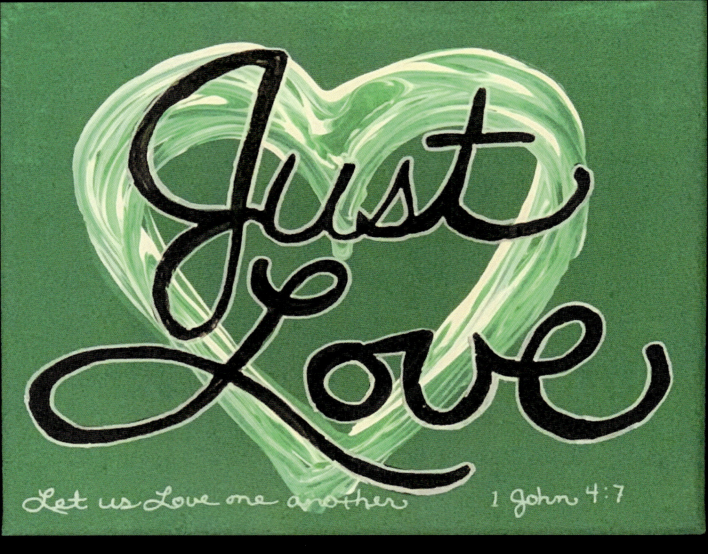

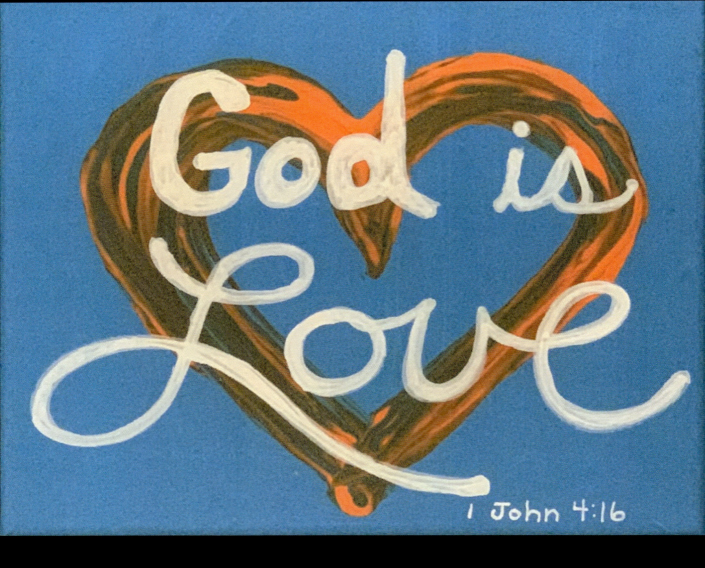

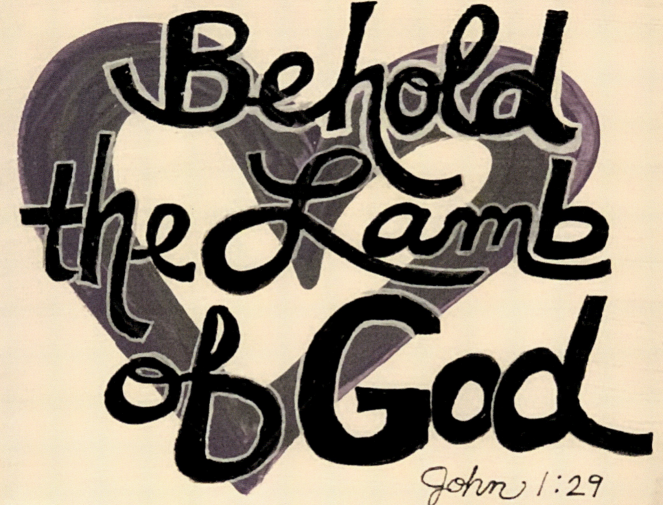

I cried out to the Lord,
He heard my voice and He
answered me.

Jonah 2:2

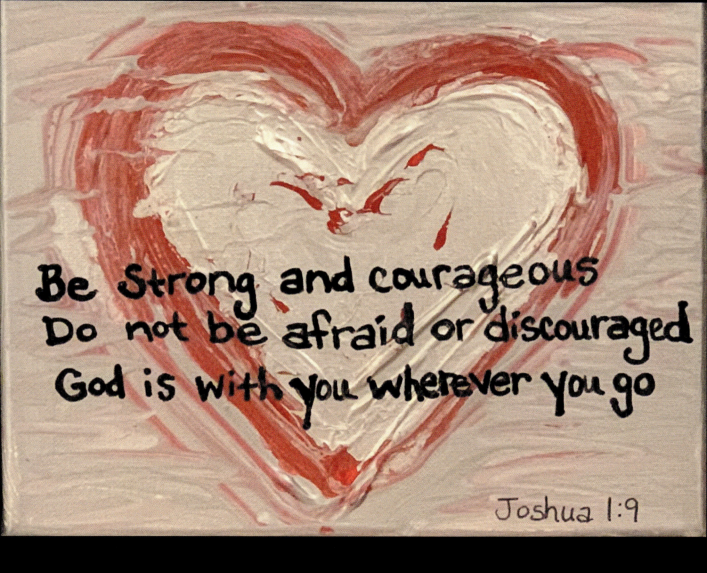

Keep yourself in God's Love as you wait for the mercy of our Lord Jesus Christ to bring you eternal Life

Jude 1:21

God gave you a wise and discerning mind.

Kings 3:12

Your name is written in Heaven

Luke 10:20

Rejoice that your name is written in Heaven

Luke 10:20

His angels will lift you up in their hands.

Luke 4:11

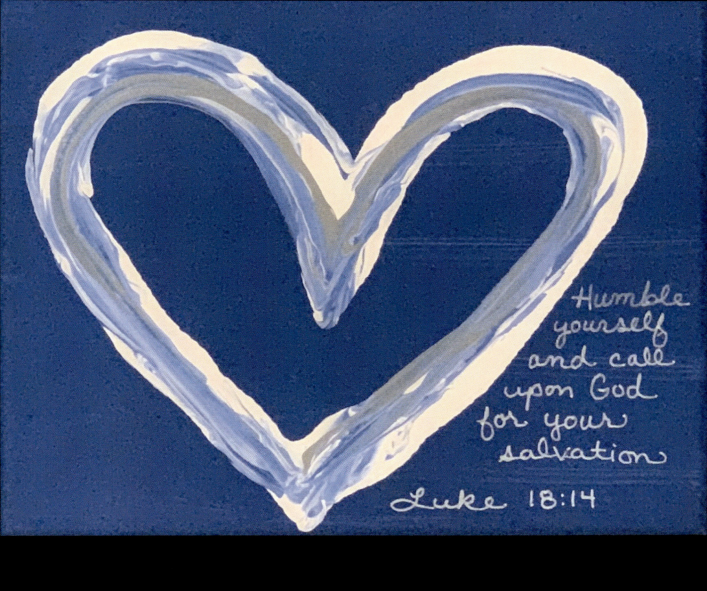

Give Thanks

Luke 9:16

Look up to heaven and give thanks ♡

He will command His angels to carefully guard you

Luke 4:10

Be a Servant of All

Mark 9:35

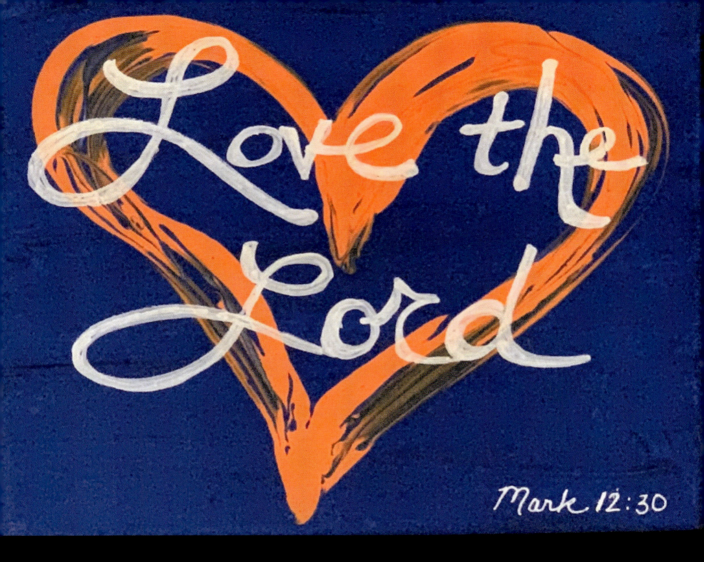

Love the Lord with all your Heart

Mark 12:30

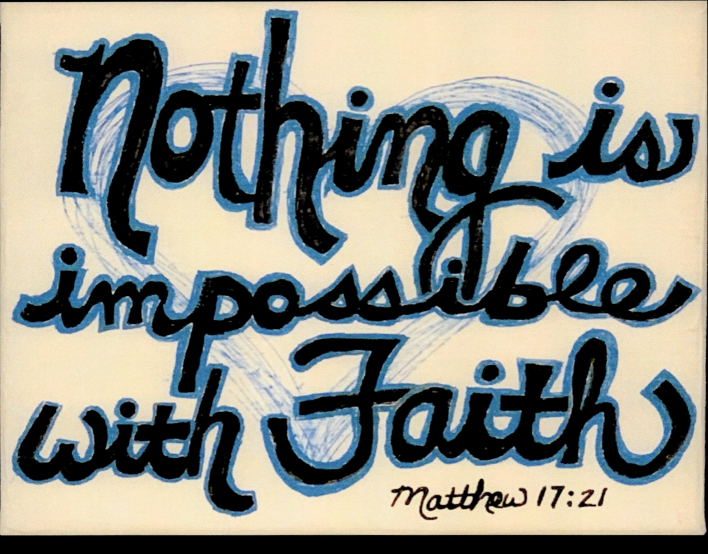

Come to me all you who are weary and burdened and I will give you rest

Matthew 11:28

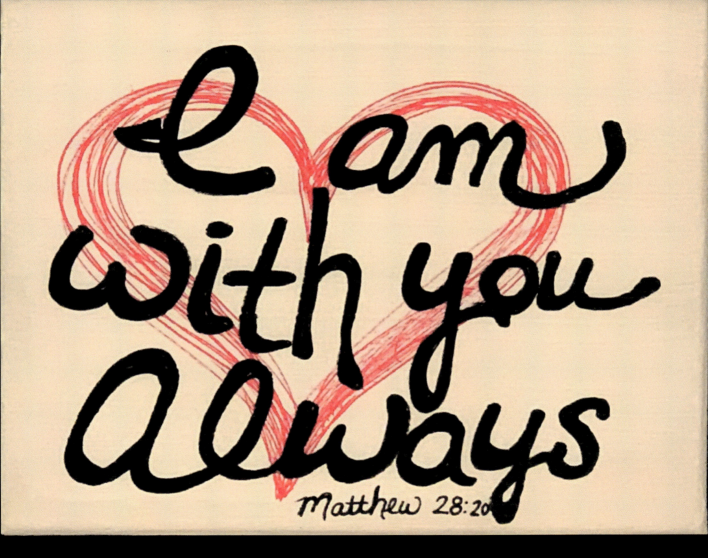

Everyone who asks will Receive

Matthew 7:8

Let your good deeds shine so that everyone will glorify and praise the Lord

Matthew 5:16

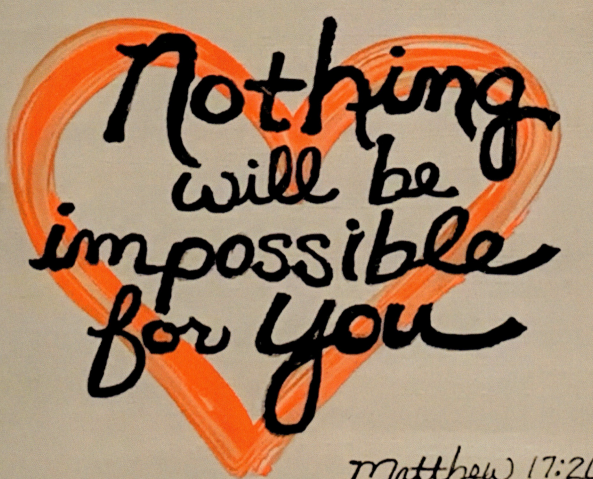

For you who Love the Lord the sun of righteousness will rise with healing in its rays

Malachi 4:2

The Lord is good. He is a refuge in times of trouble. He cares for those who trust in Him. Nahum 1:7

The Joy of the Lord is your Strength

Nehemiah 8:10

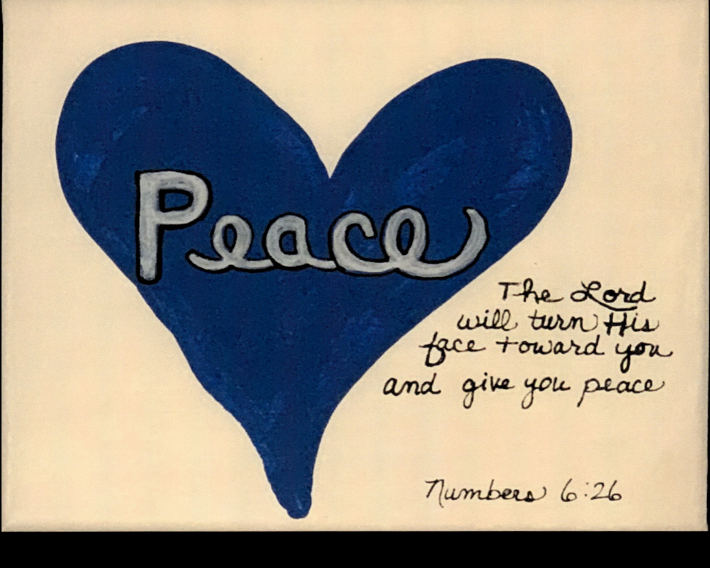

The Kingdom will belong to The Lord

Obadiah 1:21

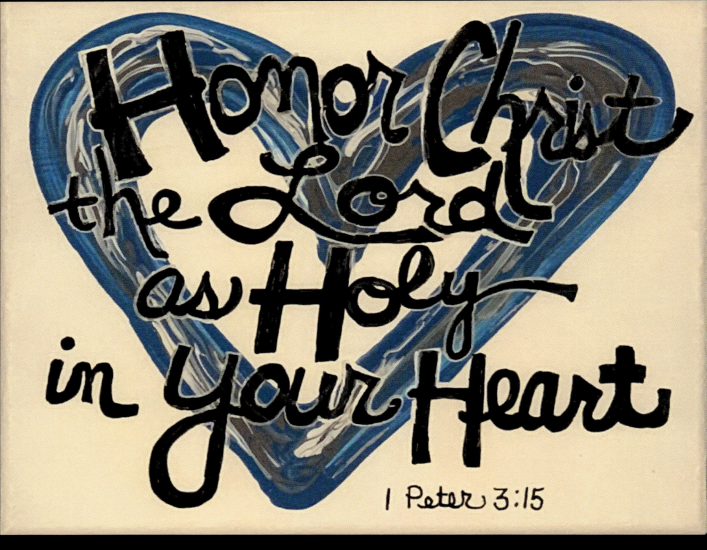

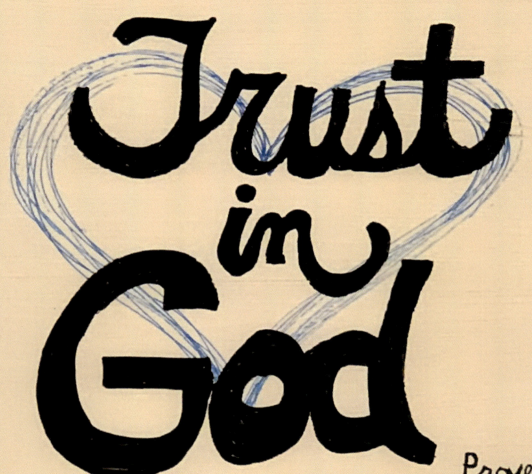

She is more precious than rubies. Nothing you desire can compare with her

Proverbs 3:15

> Train up your children in the way that they should go and when they are old they will not depart from it
>
> Proverbs 22:6

A Wise Woman puts God first

Proverbs 3:6

Entrust your works to the Lord and your plans will succeed

Proverbs 16:3

God's words give us Life

Proverbs 3:1

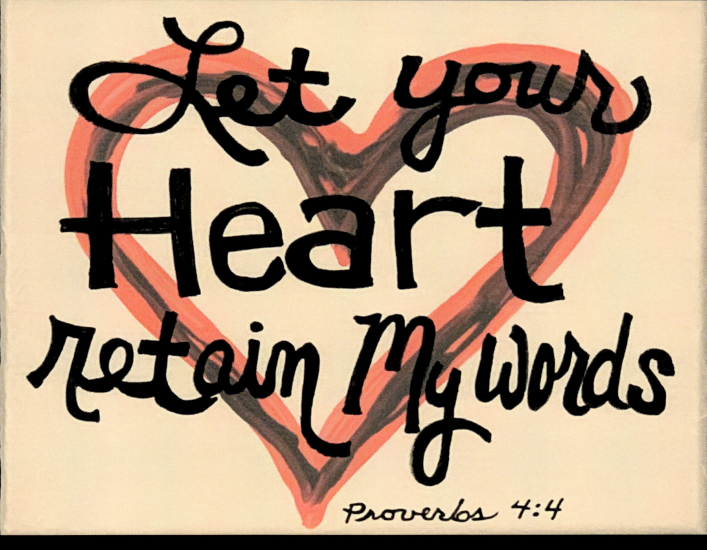

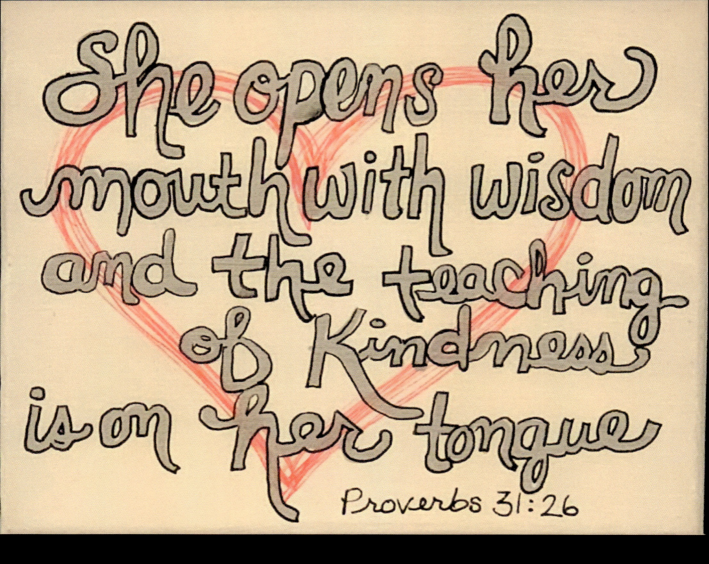

She speaks with Wisdom, Faithfulness and Kindness

Proverbs 31:26

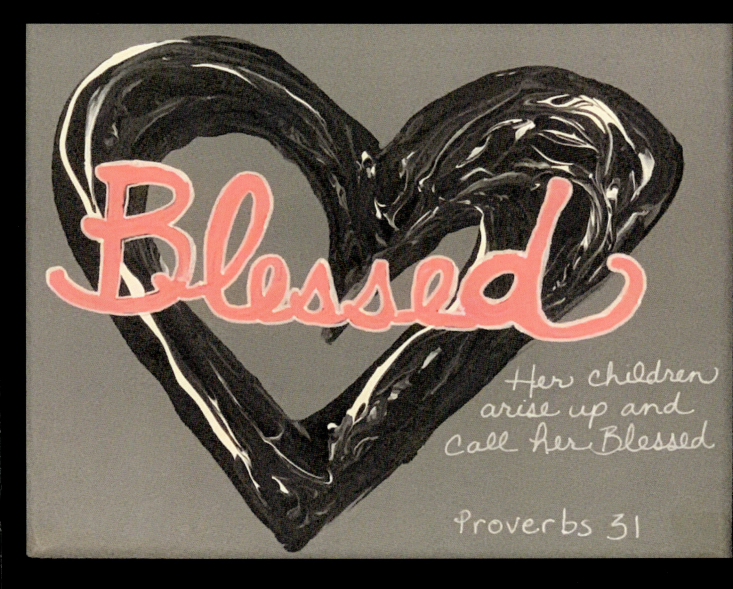

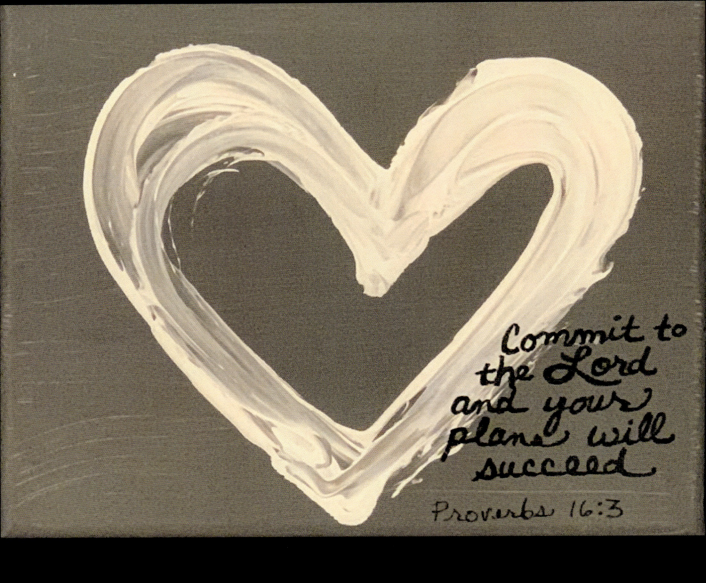

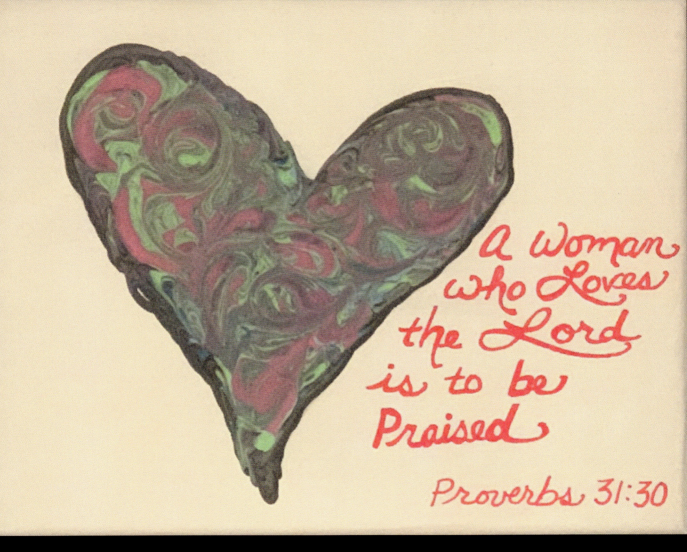

He will show you which path to take

Proverbs 3:6

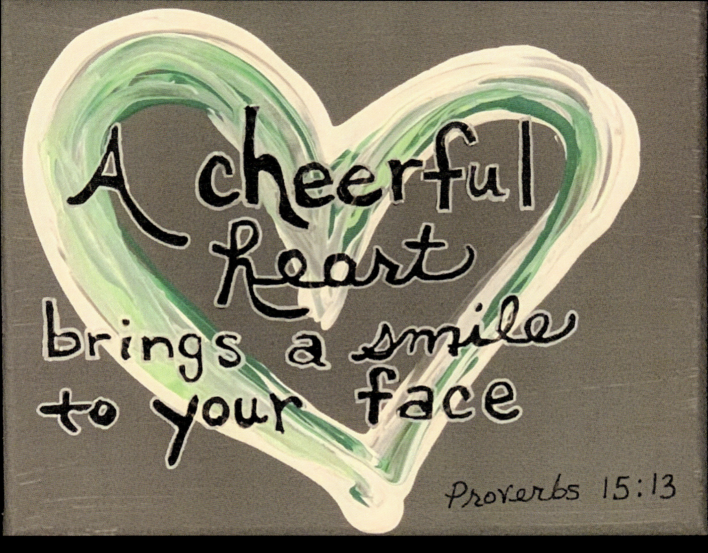

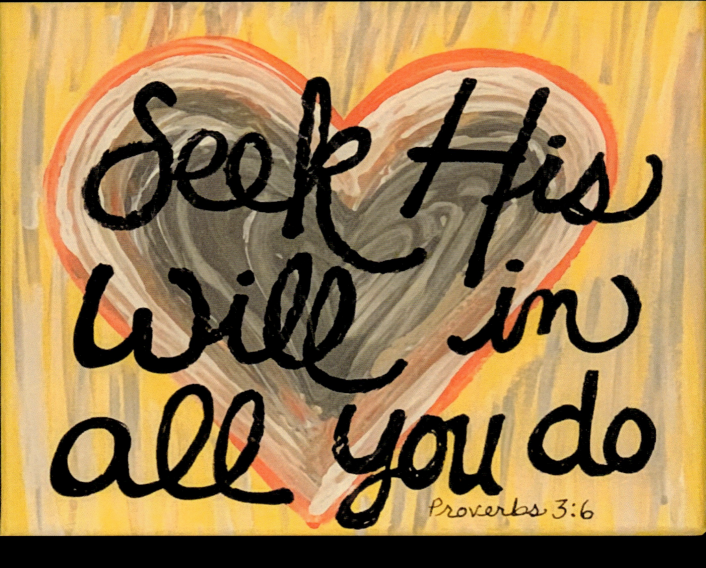

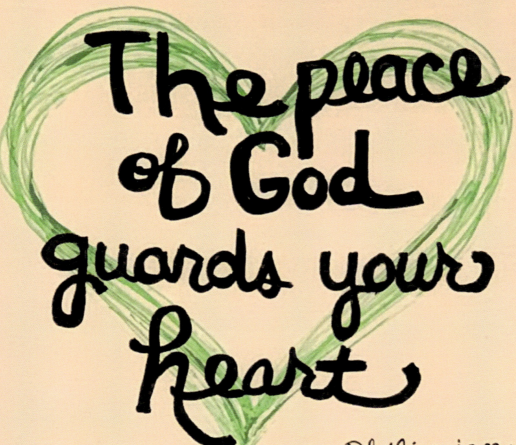

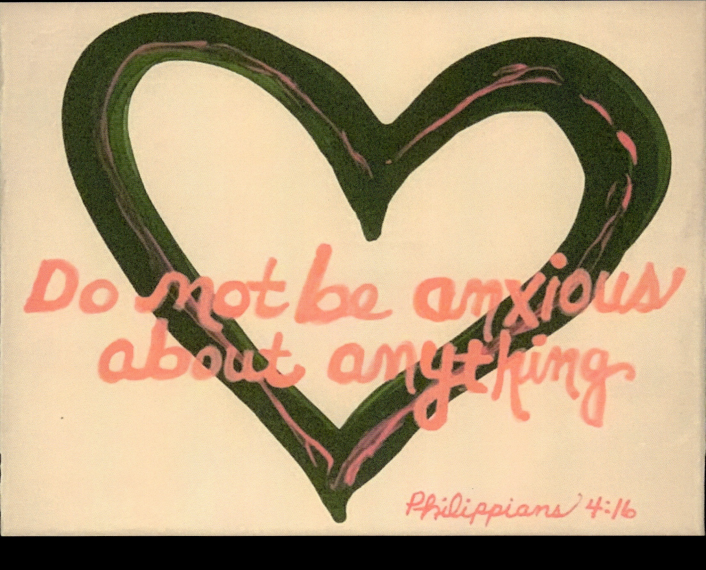

Do not harm the land, sea or trees

Revelation 7:3

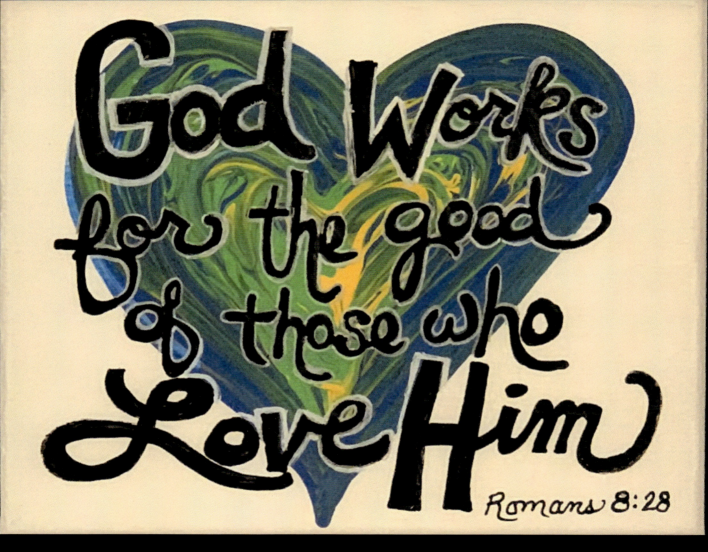

Live in Harmony with one another

Romans 12:16

May the Lord reward you for your kindness

Ruth 1:8

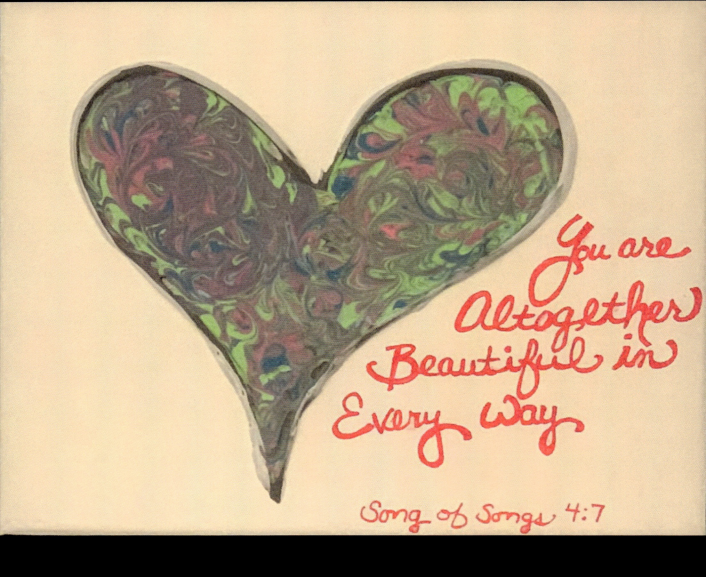

Encourage and build each other up

Thessalonians 5:11

The Kindness and Love of God our Savior appeared

Titus 3:4

I call to the Lord who is worthy of praise and I am saved

2 Samuel 22:4

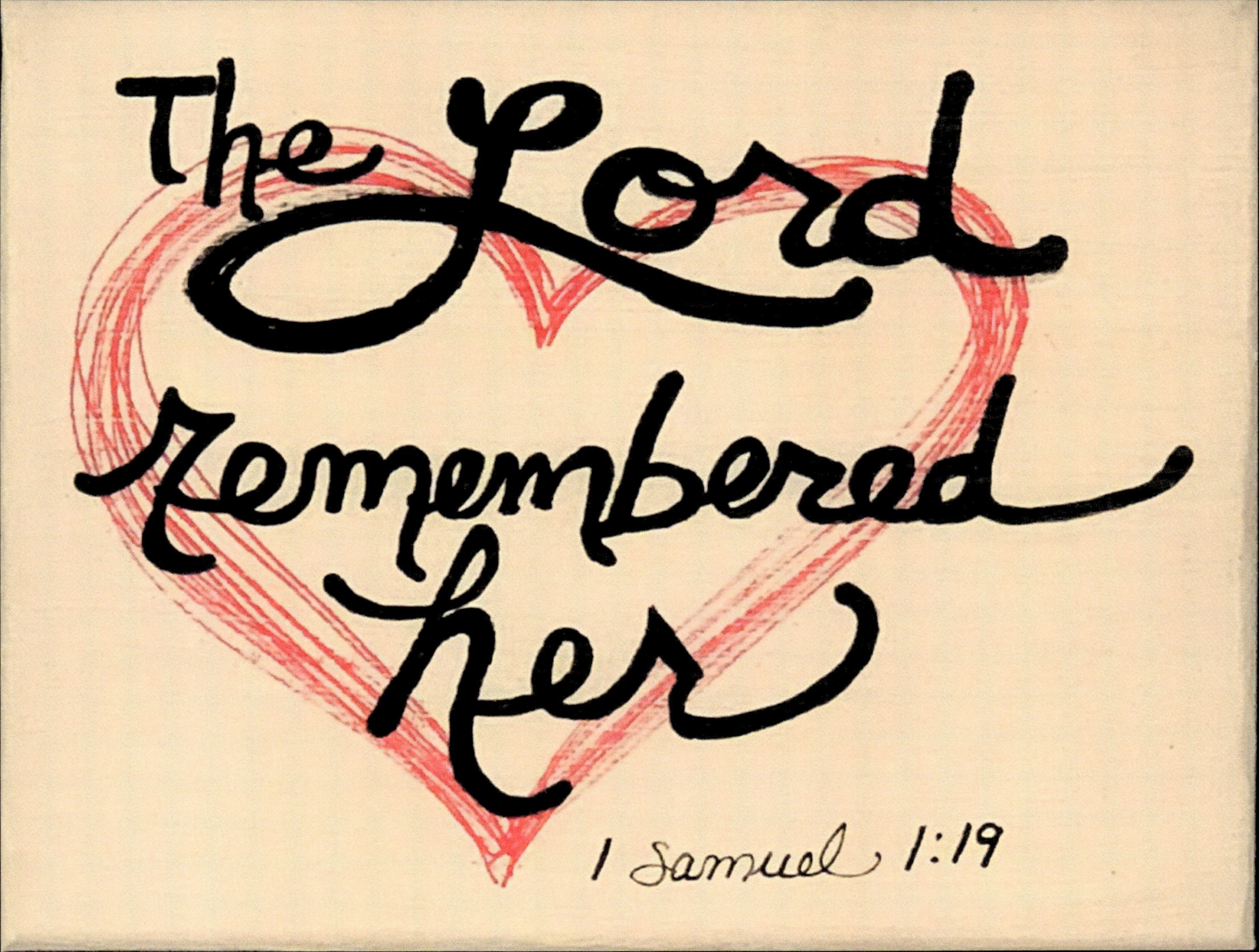

The Lord remembered her

1 Samuel 1:19

The Lord will save His people They will sparkle like jewels in a crown

Zechariah 9:16

The Lord will Rejoice over you with shouts of Joy.

Zephaniah 3:17

The Lord your God is with you. He will take great delight in you. He will rejoice over you with singing.

Zephaniah 3:17

Happy are those whose delight is in the Law of the Lord and on His Law they meditate day and night

Psalm 1:1-2

> You have filled my Heart with Greater Joy
>
> Psalm 4:7

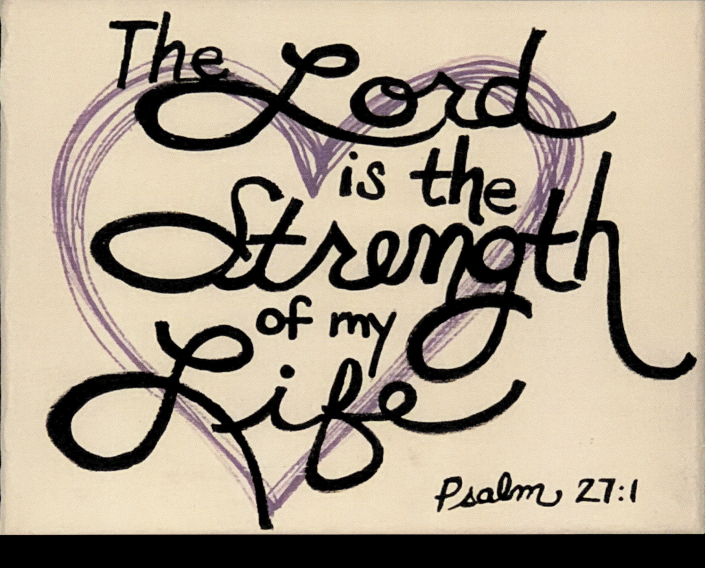

You turned my wailing into dancing;
You removed my sackcloth and
    clothed me with joy,
that my heart may sing to you and
                not be silent.
O Lord my God, I will give you thanks forever!
Psalm 30:11-12   Amen

To God be all the glory for all the great things He has done in my Life I am truly thankful I will praise the Lord at all times

Psalm 34:1

God is within her
She will not fail

Psalm 46:5

I will remember the deeds of the Lord; yes I will remember Your miracles of long ago. I will meditate on all Your works and consider all your mighty deeds.

Psalm 77:11-12

This is the day the Lord has made Let us Rejoice and be glad in it

Psalm 118:24

Please do not give up on me

Psalm 119:8

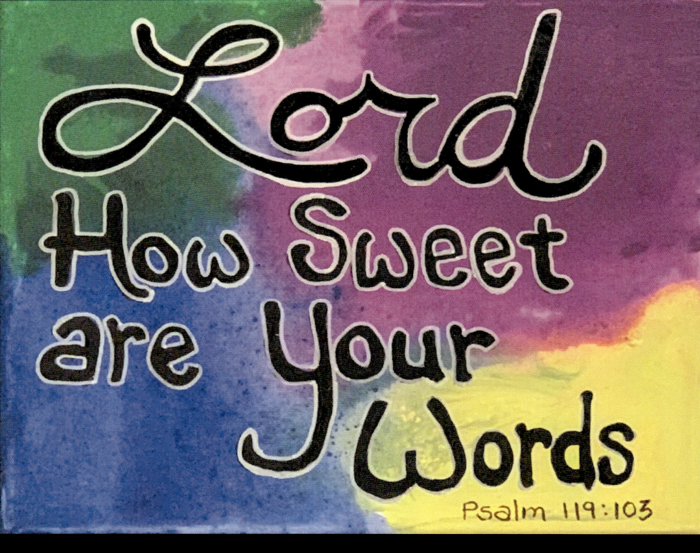

The Lord Remembered His Holy Word

Psalm 105:42

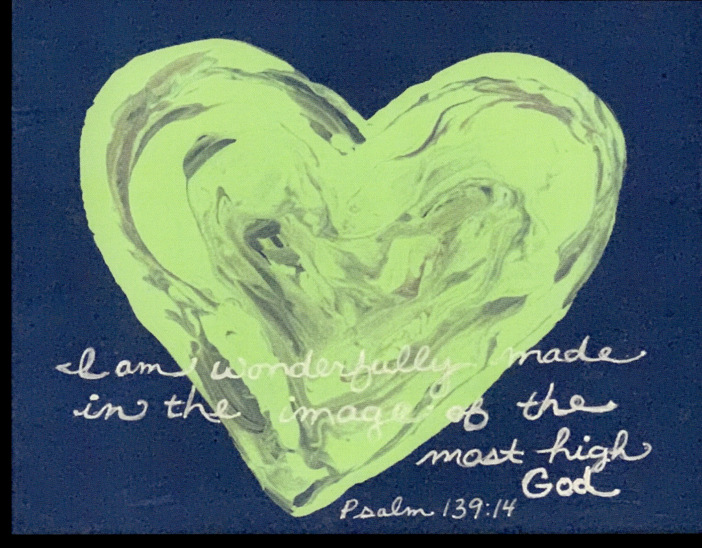

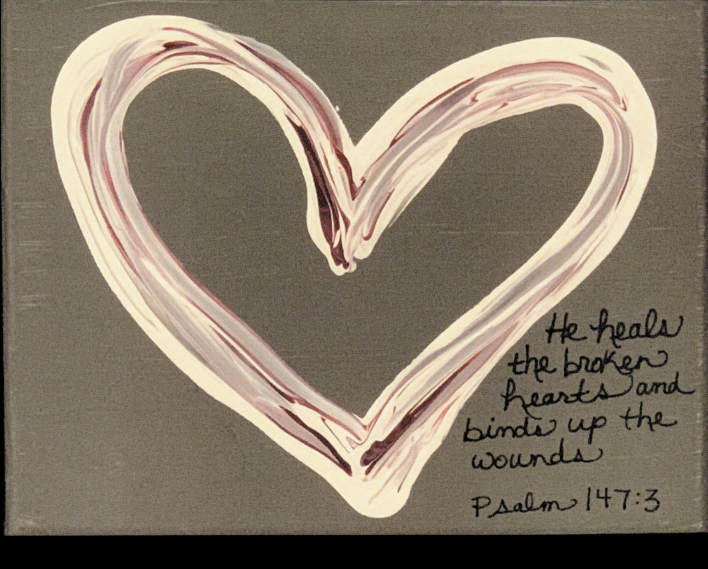

He has done Great Things

Joel 2:20

God is the only one who can make the valley of trouble a door of hope

Hosea 2:15

Fear not because your God will come with vengeance and save you

Isaiah 35:4

The Word of God is alive and powerful

Hebrews 4:12

The Sovereign Lord is my Strength

Habakkuk 3:19

Find Grace in the Eyes of The Lord

Genesis 6:8

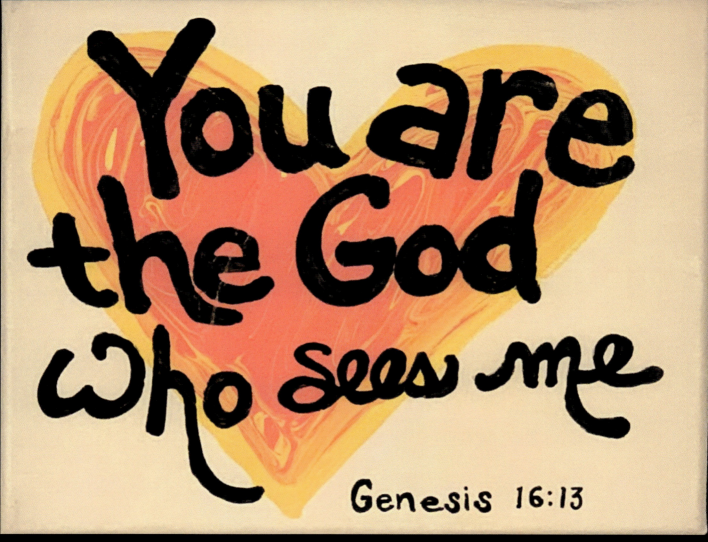

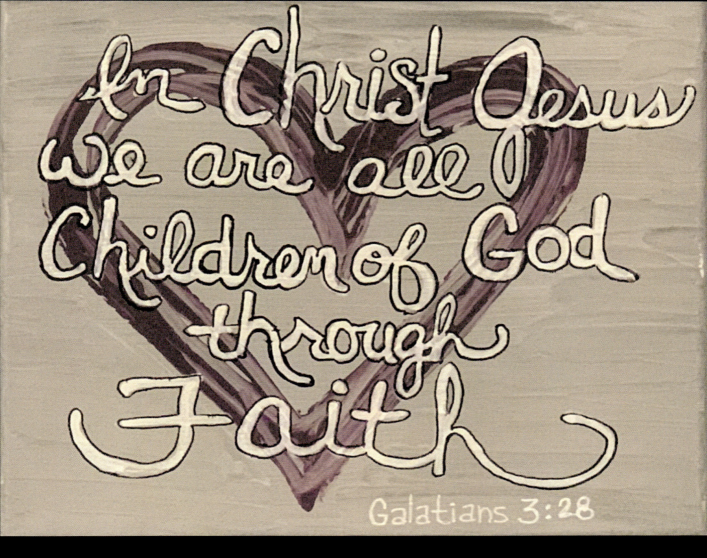

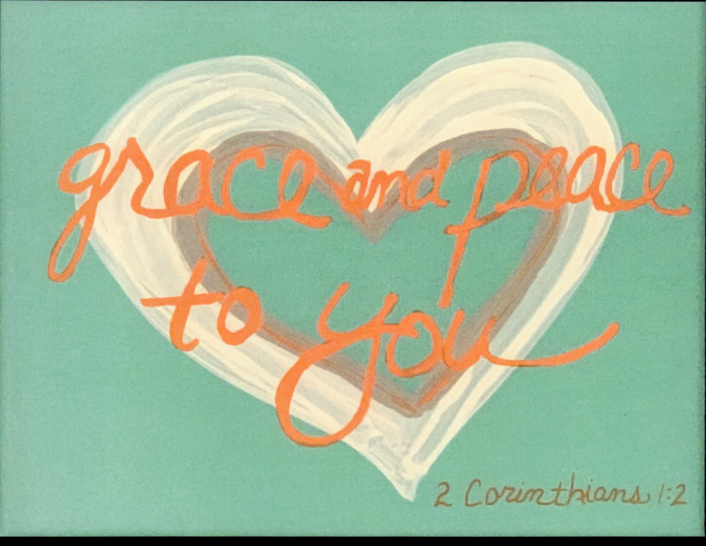

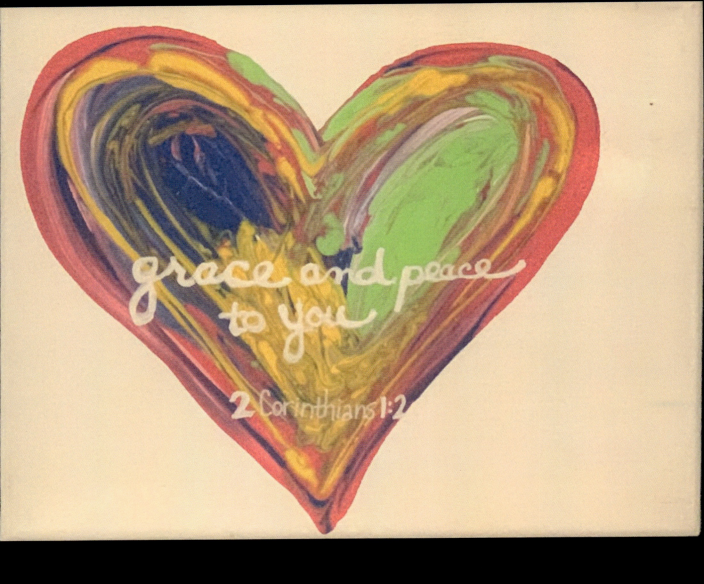

Let the Peace of Christ rule in your Heart

Colossians 3:15

Let us do our best to know the Lord. He will refresh us like rain renewing the Earth in the Springtime.

Hosea 6:3

Live a Life filled with Love

Ephesians 5:2

God has heard your prayer

Luke 1:13

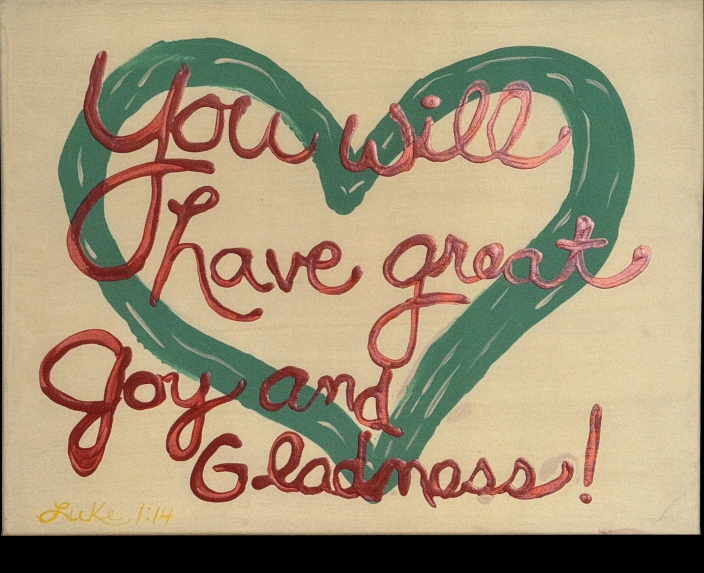

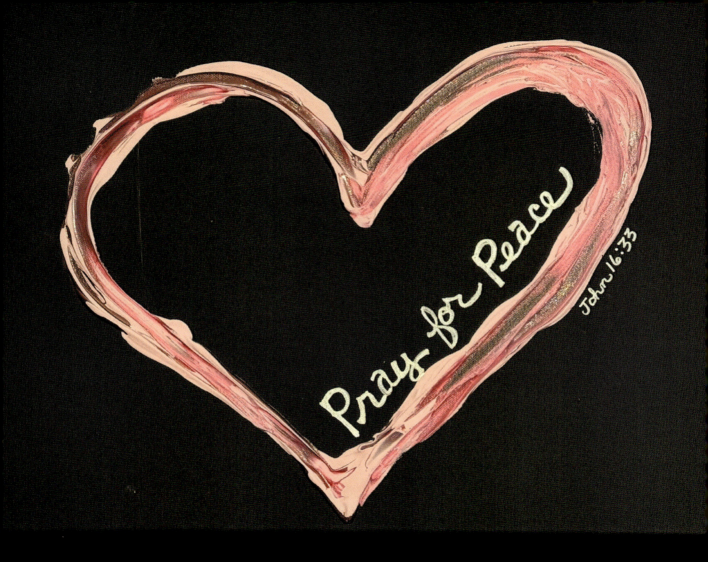

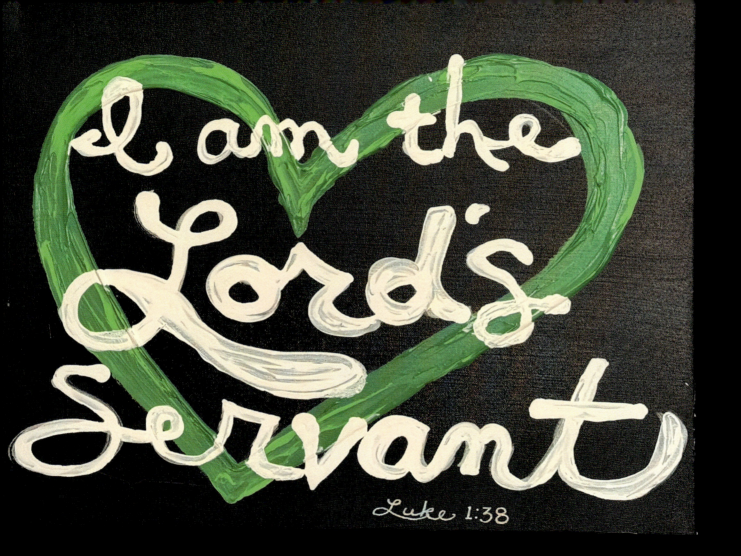

Be Completely Humble and Gentle
Be Patient
Bearing One Another in Love

Ephesians 4:2

Throughout My Life My God Has Been Faithful

Psalm 116

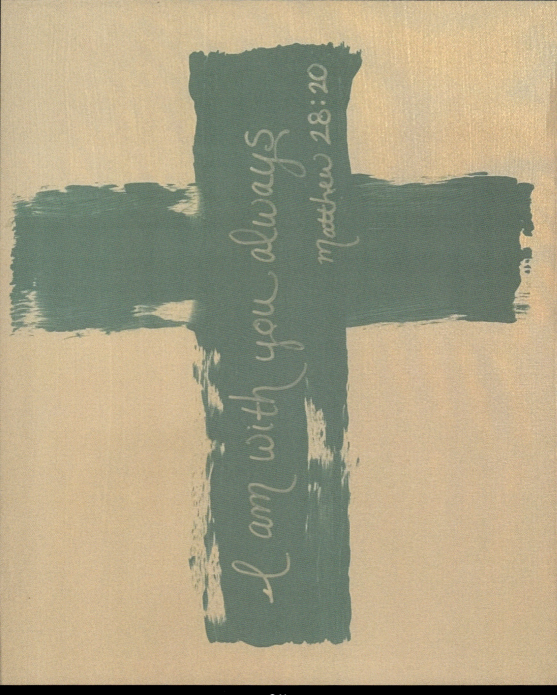

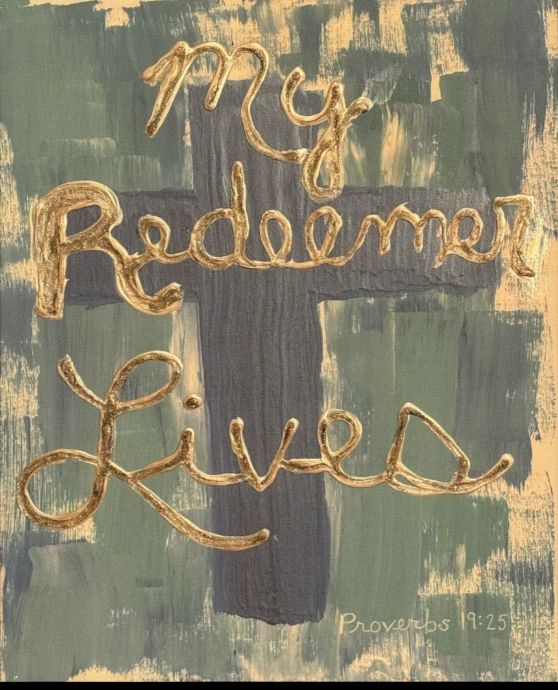

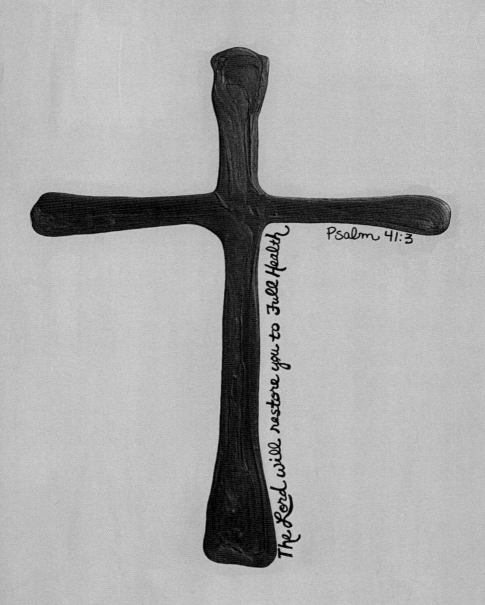

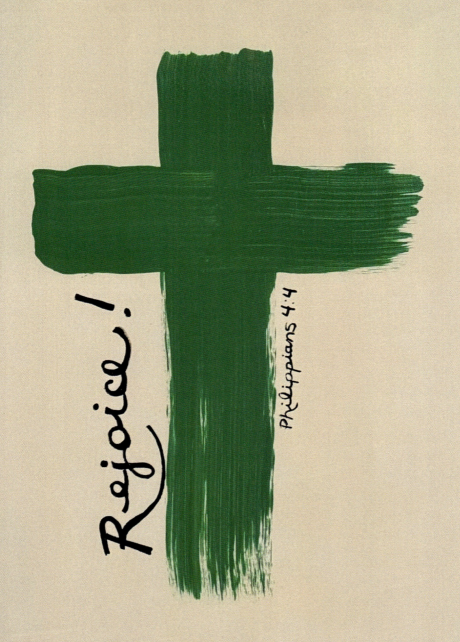

Praise the Lord

Psalm 135:3

A Sweet friendship Refreshes the Soul

Proverbs 27:9

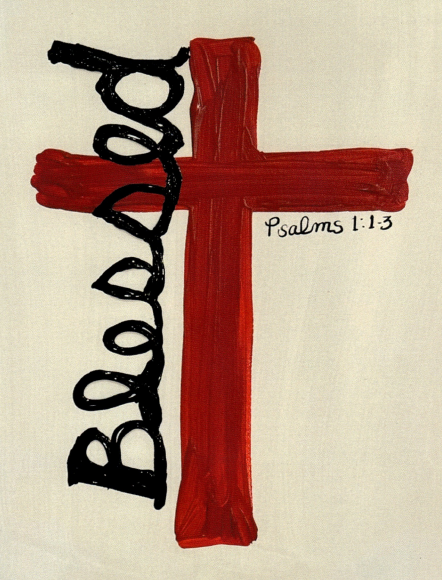

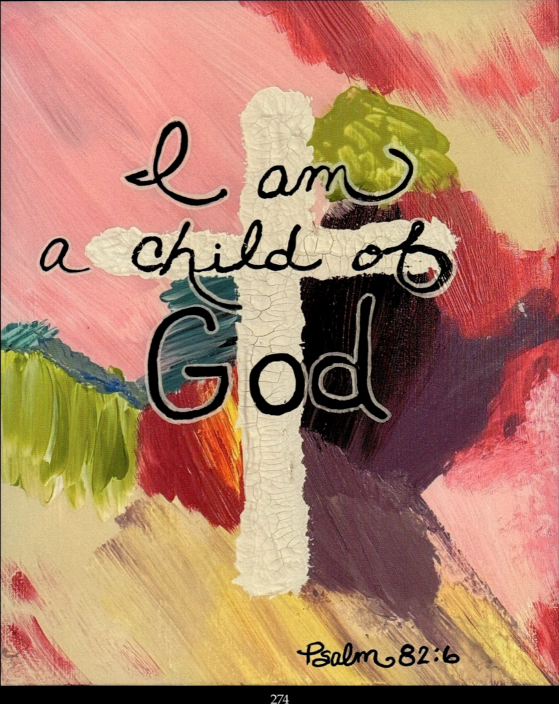

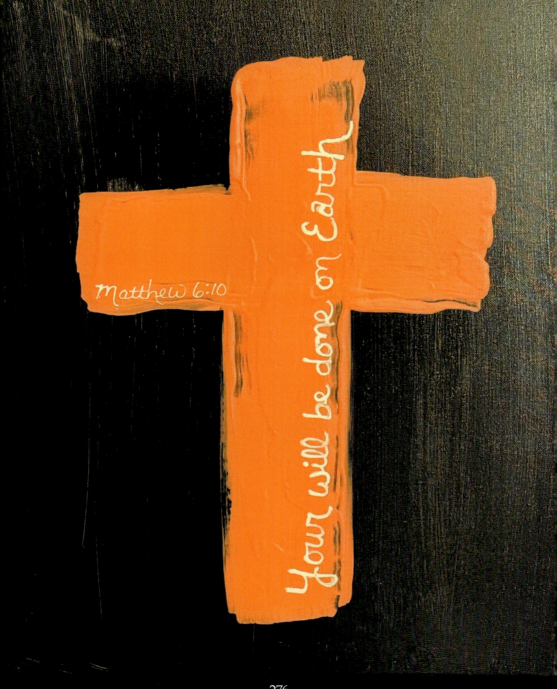

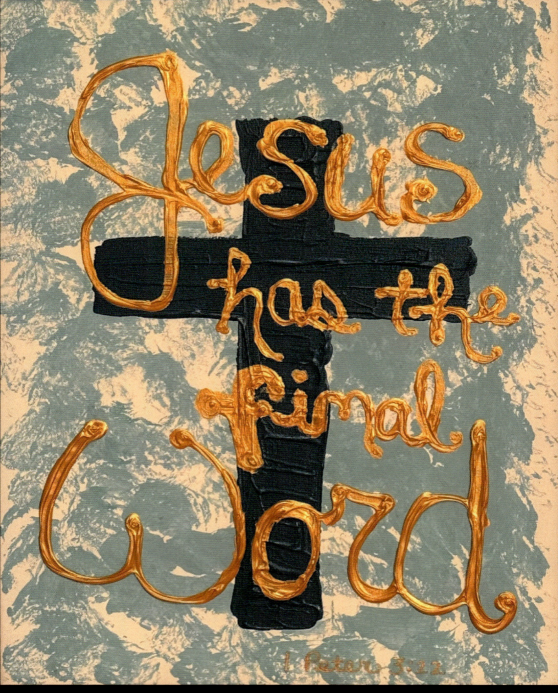

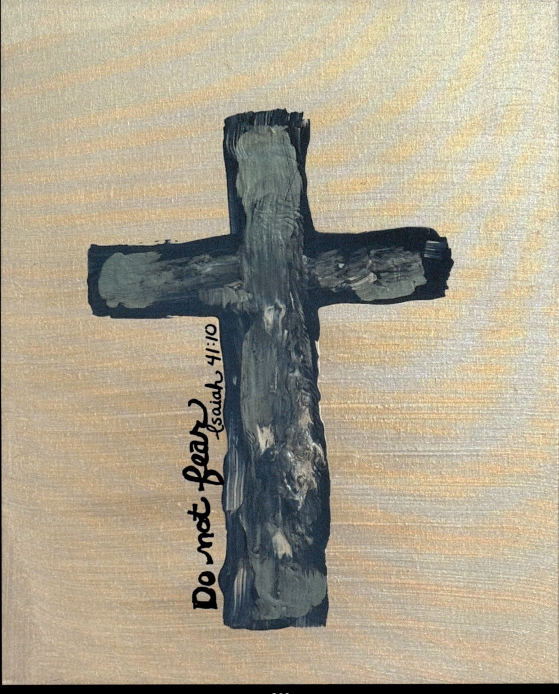

I will be confident

Psalm 27:3

It is Well With My Soul

John 14:27

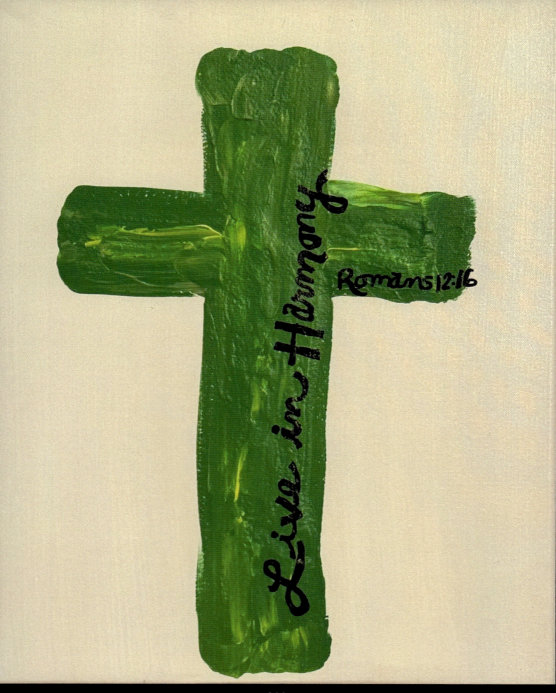

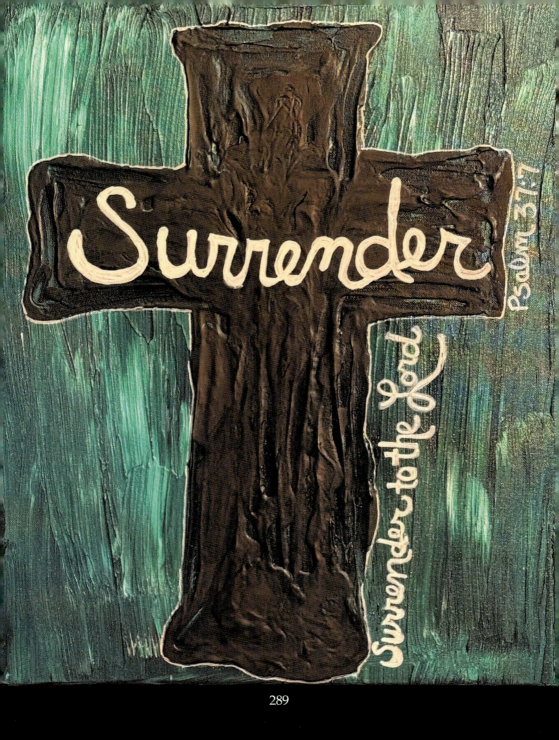

Grace is a Gift from God — Ephesians 2:8

You give me courage. Psalm 34:

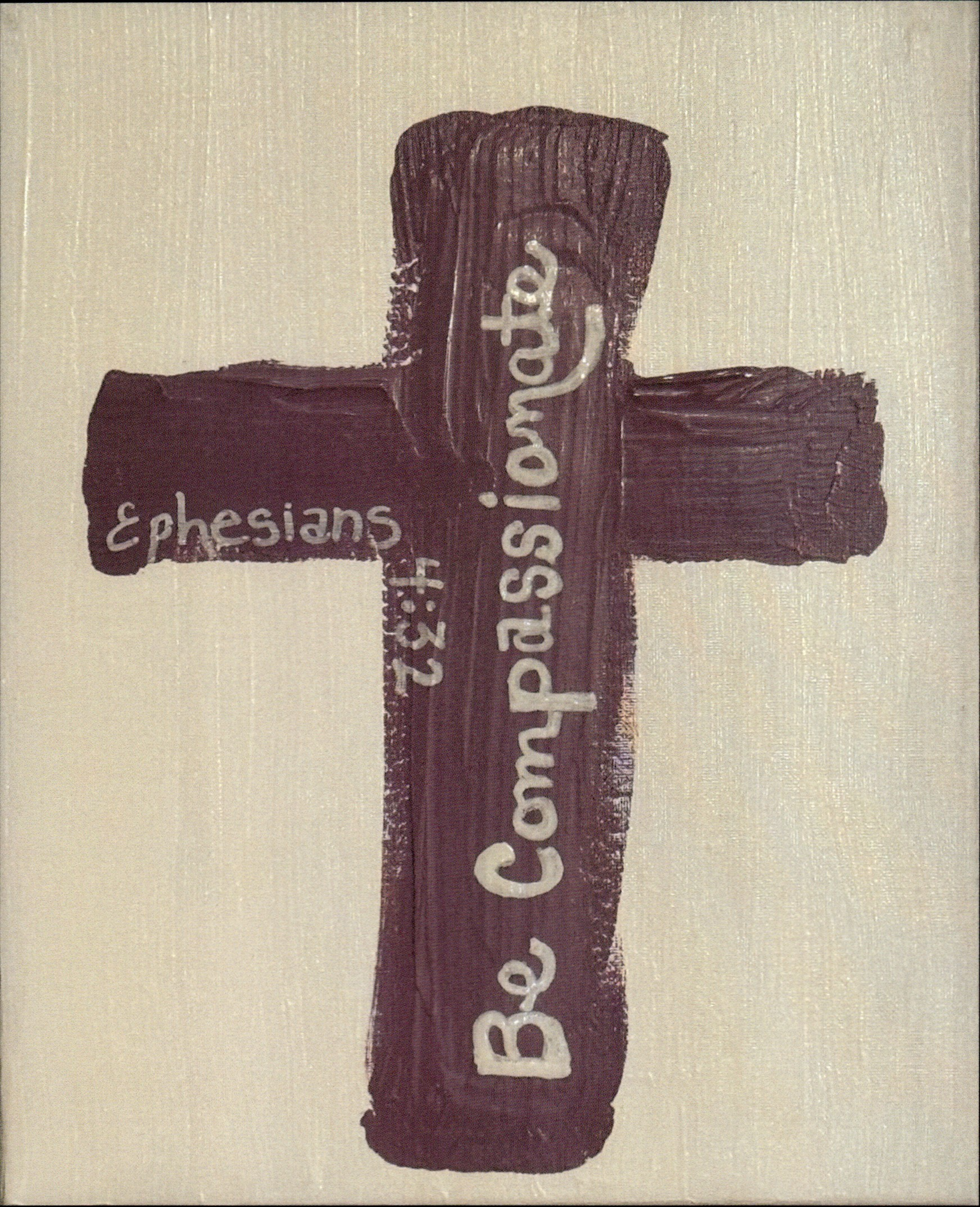

Be Compassionate

Ephesians 4:32

Rejoice in Hope

Romans 12:12

Well done good and faithful servant

Matthew 25:23